# THE WORLD'S SHORTEST BOOKS

# THE WORLD'S SHORTEST BOOKS

## FROM
# DAVID FROST
## ON SUNDAY

### WITH MEL CALMAN · MICHAEL HEATH · BILL TIDY · WILLIAM RUSHTON

Do you know who I am? .... No!

**Collins/FONTANA**

First published in 1987 by Fontana Paperbacks
A division of the Collins Publishing Group
8 Grafton Street, London W1

Copyright © David Paradine Productions 1987

Made and printed in Great Britain
by William Collins Sons & Co Ltd, Glasgow

# ACKNOWLEDGEMENTS

This book – and its proceeds – is dedicated to the families of all those who suffered in the Enniskillen bomb outrage.

There are so many people who have made this book possible. I would like to thank them all. First, Mrs Doris Hadden of Bromley, who made the telephone call on Sunday, November 15th to suggest the idea of a book of *The World's Shortest Books*, an idea about which I was instantly enthused there and then, on the air.

Then Ian Chapman, Chairman of Collins, who I rang that Sunday morning; and Eddie Bell, Managing Director of Collins who followed up on Monday. "If I have the text and illustrations with you in a week's time, I'd like to have a book in the shop within two weeks," I said to him. "It's impossible," said Eddie, "but we'll do it."

I'd like to thank our superb illustrators: Mel Calman, Michael Heath, Willie Rushton and Bill Tidy, who – with all the massive demands on their time – gave me an instant 'yes' that same afternoon.

I would also like to salute the generosity of the *Sunday Times*, Andrew Neil, Michael Cranmer and their Photo Library for providing their photographs to this book at no charge.

Thanks are also due to all the viewers of *David Frost on Sunday* who have come up with so many marvellous ideas for this book, and to Fred Metcalf, Mary Ann Madden and Ben Ramos for their additional stop-press efforts.

Finally, I would like to thank you, gentle reader, for investing in this book, and infiltrate, if I may, the respectful suggestion that it might be a *terrific* idea to buy another dozen copies as Christmas presents!

Thank you again

DAVID FROST

# THE WONDERFUL
# WORLD OF
# HANG GLIDING
by Cyril Smith

HE FLEW TOO NEAR THE SUN
AND EVERY CHIP SHOP IN
ROCHDALE!

# LET'S MISBEHAVE
by Mother Teresa
of Calcutta

# COMING
# TO TERMS
# WITH
# CHARISMA
by Robert
McLennan

# JOB
# SATISFACTION
# AT THE BBC
by Michael Grade

LIFE IN MY
HUSBAND'S SHADOW
by Mrs Denis Thatcher

**POST WAR GERMANY**
by Rudolf Hess

**SWEEPING TO VICTORY**
by Mike Gatting

IN PRAISE OF
OLDER WOMEN
by
Roman Polanski

# BRINGING UP CHILDREN
## by W C Fields

# ADOLF HITLER:
# MY PART IN HIS DOWNFALL
## by Kurt Waldheim

## FOOLING AROUND
by Victoria Gillick

## BRIEF ENCOUNTER
by
Anatoly Karpov
and
Gary Kasparov

## I BELIEVE
by the Bishop
of Durham

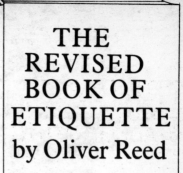

THE
REVISED
BOOK OF
ETIQUETTE
by Oliver Reed

**PARLIAMENTARY
ETIQUETTE**
by Dennis Skinner

THE KAMA SUTRA:
A RE-APPRAISAL
by
Cliff Richard

# THE COMPLETE GUIDE
# TO BARMITZVAH TOASTS
by Yasser Arafat

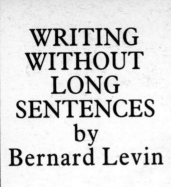

WRITING
WITHOUT
LONG
SENTENCES
by
Bernard Levin

INTERVIEWING
WITHOUT LONG
SENTENCES
by Peter Jay

**AMERICA ON
20 DOLLARS A DAY**
by Imelda Marcos

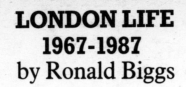

**LONDON LIFE
1967-1987**
by Ronald Biggs

**THE
HIGHWAY
CODE**
by James Dean

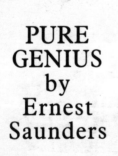

PURE
GENIUS
by
Ernest
Saunders

# A PROFESSIONAL GUIDE TO GRAFFITI
## by Michelangelo

LIFE AT NUMBER 10
by Neil Kinnock

HANGOVER
CURES

by King Fahd

THE C5 AT
LE MANS:
THE GLORY
YEARS
by Sir Clive
Sinclair

# INDUSTRIAL DEMOCRACY –
# THE WAY FORWARD
## by Rupert Murdoch

## THE VATICAN GUIDE TO GUILT-FREE SEX

LORD LUCAN'S
PUBLIC
ENGAGEMENTS,
1987-8

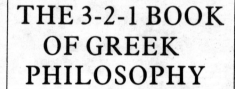

THE 3-2-1 BOOK
OF GREEK
PHILOSOPHY

# WINDSURFING IN THE STRAITS OF HORMUZ

# 14-17: THE YEARS OF INNOCENCE
## by Mandy Smith

## WHAT TO DO WHEN YOUR GIRO HASN'T COME
by the Sultan of Brunei

## IMAGINATIVE CAKE COOKERY FOR ALL
by
Alfred
the Great

## ON THE ROAD TO MATURITY
by Tony Blackburn

EAT, DRINK
AND
BE MERRY

by

Sir Keith Joseph

# MY DEFENCE ON JUDGMENT DAY

by Judas Iscariot

# UNDERSTANDING FOOTBALL REFEREES
by Mark Dennis

## CYCLING THROUGH HARLEM
by P W Botha

## TEETH CARE
by Jocky Wilson

## ELOCUTION MADE EASY – A MANUAL
by Derek Jameson
(With a foreword by Janet Street-Porter)

**MY TOP TEN
SCOTTISH
GOALKEEPERS**
by Jimmy Greaves

**MY LIFE
WITHOUT
JIMMY GREAVES**
by Ian St John

**A PICTORIAL
GUIDE TO
SWEDISH
CINEMA**
by Mary Whitehouse

# OUI
## by
## Charles
## de Gaulle

# THE HITE REPORT
by Steve Cauthen

# THE RIGHT WAY TO USE YOUR TAPE RECORDER
by Richard Nixon

# THE COMPLETE GUIDE TO HANKY-PANKY
by the Earl and Countess of Longford

# HOW TO WIN FRIENDS AND INFLUENCE PEOPLE   by Derek Hatton

# GRUDGE MATCH
by Teddy Johnson
and Pearl Carr

# FEAR OF FLYING
by David Frost

# SILENCE IS GOLDEN
by Murray Walker

# THE PROFESSIONAL DARTS ASSOCIATION BOOK OF HEALTH & BEAUTY

180!

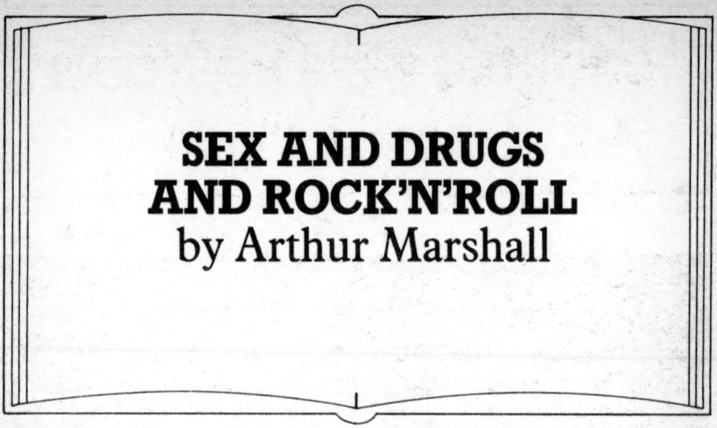

**SEX AND DRUGS
AND ROCK'N'ROLL**
by Arthur Marshall

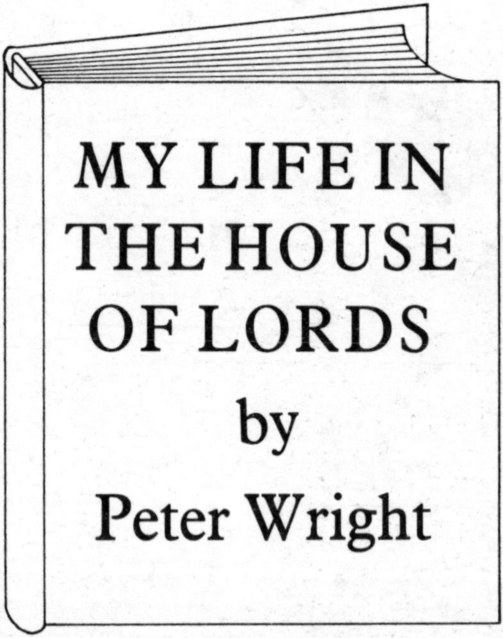

MY LIFE IN
THE HOUSE
OF LORDS

by

Peter Wright

# COOKING WITH DOLPHINS
## by Jacques Cousteau

**MUD WRESTLING:
A HISTORY**
by Barbara Cartland

OUR CRAZY
LEGAL
SYSTEM
by
Sir Michael
Havers

THAT WHICH CANNOT
BE BOUGHT
by Gerald Ronson

# LOVE AND THE LIBERATED WOMAN
## by Ayatollah Khomeni

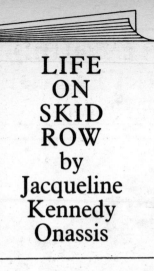

**LIFE
ON
SKID
ROW
by
Jacqueline
Kennedy
Onassis**

**THE WOMEN
IN MY LIFE**
by Harvey Proctor

HOUSE BUYING IN
PLYMOUTH

by David Steel

# LEADERS I WOULD
# HAPPILY SERVE UNDER
## by David Owen

**HOW TO MAKE IT BIG
ON YOUR OWN**
by Nancy Sinatra

**STAND BY
YOUR MAN**
by Simon Peter

THE MAGIC OF THE
ROYALS
by Willie Hamilton

# MY SECRET LIFE
## by Joan Collins

# HOW TO
# IMPRESS
# YOUR
# EMPLOYER
by
Tommy Docherty

## THE ART OF COMPROMISE
by Linda Bellos

## MY ONE HUNDRED
## BEST PARTY JOKES

by Tony Benn

# TEACH YOURSELF RUGBY LEAGUE
by Boy George

## CHIPS WITH EVERYTHING
by
Edwina Currie

## LOVE THY NEIGHBOUR
by Bernie Grant

## SO YOU WANT TO BE AN OPERA SINGER
by Max Bygraves

# KEEPING OUT OF THE LIMELIGHT
## by Richard Branson

# HOLIDAYING IN THE VATICAN
## by Rev. Ian Paisley

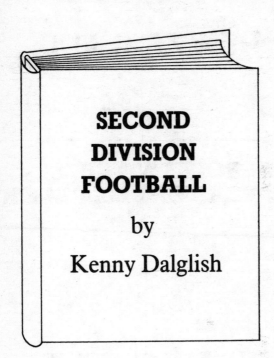

**SECOND**

**DIVISION**

**FOOTBALL**

by

Kenny Dalglish

# WHO'S WHO IN NEW ZEALAND

## NICHOLAS WITCHELL – HOT-HEAD OR HELLRAISER?

## THE FAMOUS FIVE MEET COLONEL GADDAFI

# TIMESHARE OPPORTUNITIES
## IN BEIRUT

# TACT
## by Bernard Manning

## I WAS THE FIFTH BEATLE
by Sir Georg Solti

## SELF RESTRAINT MADE EASY
by Sean Penn

## THE FREEDOM OF INFORMATION ACT EXPLAINED
by Robert Mugabe

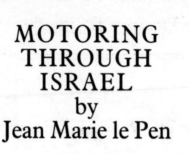

MOTORING
THROUGH
ISRAEL
by
Jean Marie le Pen

**SPYCATCHER –
THE LEGAL VERSION**
by Sir Robert Armstrong

# THE DANGERS OF
# LUNG CANCER
## by Sir Walter Raleigh

## MY BATTLE WITH SEXUAL INHIBITION
### by Bill Wyman

## SHYNESS
### by Gyles Brandreth

## MY COUNTRY, RIGHT OR WRONG
### by Ken Livingstone

# A HISTORY OF THE GILLETTE COMPANY
## by Bob Geldof

## KAMPALA REVISITED
by Idi Amin

**TENNIS RACKET CARE**
by
John McEnroe

# AFTER-DINNER SPEAKING MADE EASY
by Dave Nellist

**WEAK SPOTS
IN THE
BERLIN WALL**
by Erich Honecker

**KEEPING
YOUR FEET
ON THE
GROUND**
by Rudolf
Nureyev

SLOPPING OUT
MADE EASY
by Malcolm Rifkind

# MAKE YOUR OWN SARI
## by Enoch Powell

# CELIBACY FOR BEGINNERS
by Sir Ralph Halpern

**HONESTY IS THE BEST POLICY** by Ivan Boesky

THE GOOD FRUIT
JUICE AND
CORDIAL GUIDE
by Dean Martin

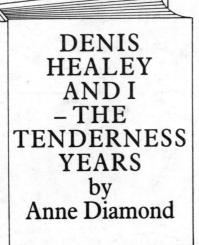

DENIS
HEALEY
AND I
– THE
TENDERNESS
YEARS
by
Anne Diamond

# MARGARET THATCHER: WOMAN OF THE CENTURY
## by Edward Heath

# THE JOY OF POLO

## by the Princess of Wales

---

**RASH BRASH
AND DEVIL-MAY-CARE!**
by Alastair Burnet

---

# THE ART OF
# GUSTAV MAHLER

## by Sylvester Stallone

# THE FUTURE OF THE WELFARE STATE
## by
## John Moore

# TILL DEATH US DO PART
## by Elizabeth Taylor

# PYRAMID
# SELLING
## by Rameses II

# TALL STORIES
## by Ronnie Corbett

## HOME PERMS MADE EASY
by Gordon Honeycombe

## PRESENTING BREAKFAST TV
## WITHOUT SAYING
## "IN A SENSE"  OR "BRIEFLY"

by Mike Morris
and Richard Keys

## THE STORY
## OF VALIUM

by Lizzie Webb

## WHEN I
## GROW UP

by

Timmy Mallett

# MY LIFE AS A STAND-UP COMIC by Jonathan Dimbleby

GETTING THE BEST
OUT OF STEREO
by
Vincent Van Gogh

THE TIME

HAS COME

by
David Owen
and
David Steel

**MODERN
ARCHITECTURE:
AN APPRECIATION**
by Prince Charles

# FISHING FOR PLEASURE
## by Captain Ahab

# KEEPING TURKEYS AS PETS
## by Bernard Matthews

# PUTTING YOUR FOOT DOWN
## by Denis Thatcher

# NOT PUTTING YOUR FOOT DOWN
## by Captain Mark Phillips

# MY UNTOLD SECRETS
## by Britt Ekland

# LIFE IN THE FAST LANE
## by the Dalai Lama

## LIFE IN
## THE SLOW LANE
## by
## David Pleat

**LOST**
**FOR WORDS**
by Brian Clough

# FOLLOWING IN
# JOHN WAYNE'S FOOTSTEPS
by Larry Grayson

# SNAKES ALIVE!
## by
## The Duchess of York

---

**CLEANING UP
THE STOCK
MARKET**
by
Horatio Bottomley

---

# IGNORANCE
# IS BLISS
by Bamber Gascoigne

DIPLOMACY
by
Norman
Tebbit

**YOURS**

**SINCERELY**
by
Bob Monkhouse

**ANOREXIA NERVOSA**
by Claire Rayner

# NEEDLEWORK AND EMBROIDERY MADE EASY
## by Frank Bruno

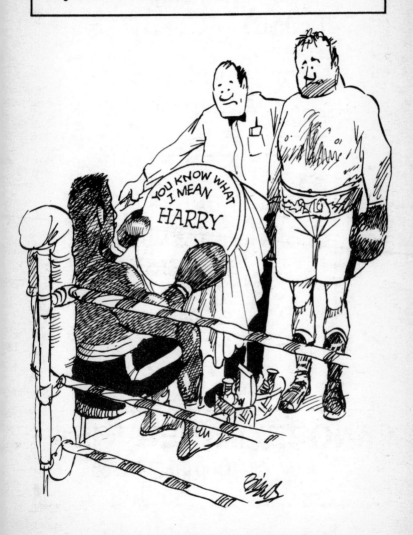

ADJUSTING TO
A NEW JOB:
THE DIFFICULTIES
by
Emperor Hirohito
of Japan

ORGANISING
A LARGE-SCALE
CONFERENCE
by
Robinson
Crusoe

TO TELL YOU
THE TRUTH . . .
by
Colonel Oliver
North

## JUST ONE OF THE LADS
### by the Duke of Westminster

## FOLLOW ME
by Mark Thatcher

## GETTING IN SHAPE
## ON A LOW BUDGET
by
Christina Onassis

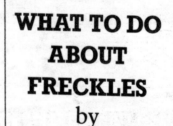

## WHAT TO DO
## ABOUT
## FRECKLES
by

Michael Jackson

GONE WITH THE WIND
by Michael Fish

# SO YOU WANT TO BE A YUPPIE?
by Mick McGahey

# MY WICKED WICKED WAYS
by Bonnie Langford

# THEY CAN'T PULL THE WOOL OVER <u>MY</u> EYES!
by Lord Dacre

# THE AGONY OF
# BEING CAMERA SHY
by Robert Maxwell

# DRESSING FOR THE OCCASION
by Michael Foot

# HOW TO GET RID OF DANDRUFF
by Duncan Goodhew

**WHY I FEAR JOE BUGNER**
by Mike Tyson

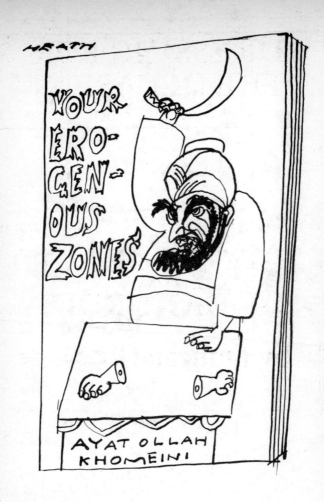

**YOUR EROGENOUS ZONES –
A PRIMER**
by Ayatollah Khomeini

**MY
BROTHER
CHRISTOPHER**
by Rusty Lee

**MY SISTER
SHIRLEY**

by

Kenneth Williams

**LIFE WITH SELINA**
by Terry Scott

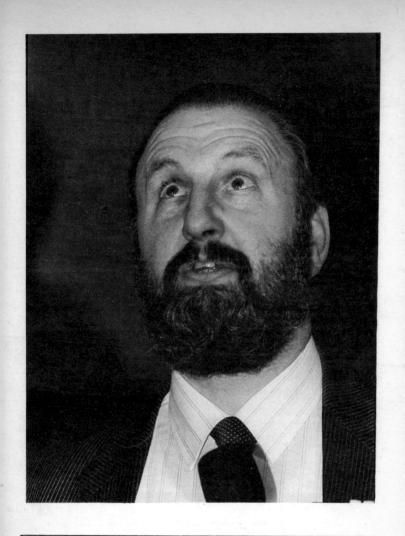

THE BEST OF GAY NEWS
by James Anderton

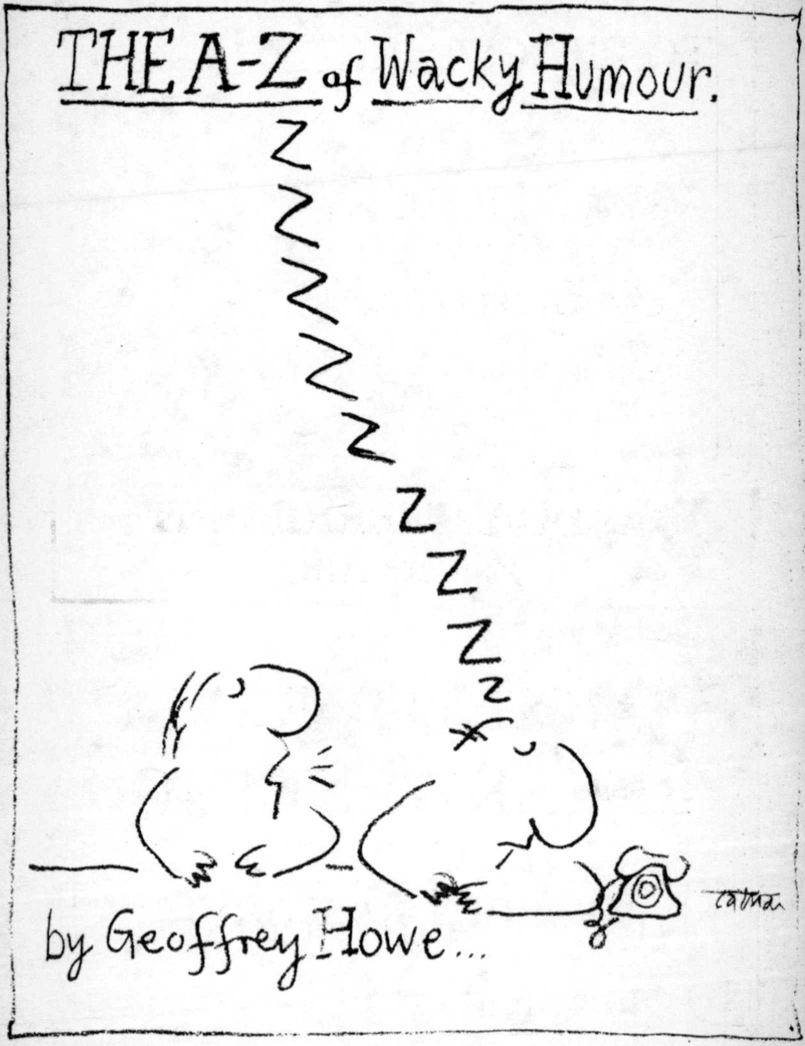
THE A-Z of Wacky Humour.
by Geoffrey Howe...

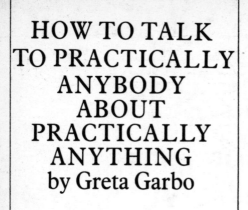

## HOW TO TALK TO PRACTICALLY ANYBODY ABOUT PRACTICALLY ANYTHING
by Greta Garbo

## MADCAP MERRIMENT
by Kate Adie

## TEACH YOURSELF BREAKDANCING

by Lord Denning

## COOKING WITHOUT WINE
by Keith Floyd

## ONE LIFE
## TO LIVE
by

Shirley Maclaine

## RETIREMENT
by
Margaret
Thatcher

MY LIFE AS
A SUMO WRESTLER
by the Archbishop of Canterbury

**REGRETS**
by
Edith Piaf

**HOW TO BE
A COMPLETE
BASTARD**
by Enid Blyton

IN DEFENCE
OF
ALTERNATIVE
LIFE-STYLES
by
Pope John Paul II

# GRATEFUL THANKS TO ALL OUR VIEWERS AND ESPECIALLY: